Dedication

This book is dedicated to all job seekers out there in the UK. Like you, I struggled often due to multiple redundancies or the Covid-19 downturn in business. It was written to help you understand the market and how hiring managers think, and I'll reveal other methods that worked for me. Whether you are still deciding between self-employment and traditional employment, this book will help you.

Preface

Unlocking Opportunities: Your Ultimate Guide to Job Hunting in the UK - A Survival Handbook is written to share my views with others who have tried and failed the Job Centre and other popular methods. As a recruitment expert, I sat on both sides of the fence, so now I'll tell you how the system works.

Succeeding in job hunting in the United Kingdom requires a strategic and informed approach. This comprehensive 10-chapter guide equips you as a reader with the understanding and skills needed to succeed as a candidate in the UK job market, from establishing a solopreneur venture to negotiating job offers and advancing one's career.

Book overview:

Chapter 1: Deciding Between Self-Employment and Traditional Employment

Whether working as a self-employed or traditionally employed worker, it Is an important decision you must make. This chapter delves into the intricacies of this decision-making process, exploring the advantages, challenges, and considerations associated with each path. Understanding the nuances between self-employment and traditional employment is crucial, as it shapes one's career trajectory, financial stability, work-life balance, and overall satisfaction.

Chapter 2: Identifying Your Skills and Career Goals

In the quest for a fulfilling career in the United Kingdom, self-awareness becomes the compass guiding individuals toward opportunities that align with their unique strengths and aspirations. Chapter two is a pivotal point in this journey, offering a roadmap for readers to identify their skills and clarify their career goals.

Chapter 3: Navigating UK Job Search Platforms

As the digital landscape becomes integral to job searches, chapter three provides insights into navigating popular UK job search platforms. From crafting effective online profiles to utilising advanced search features, readers learn how to maximise these tools to uncover relevant opportunities and streamline their job search process.

Chapter 4: Crafting a Winning UK Resume and Cover Letter

Chapter four is dedicated to crafting compelling resumes and cover letters tailored to the UK job market. From adapting to UK standards to showcasing achievements and tailoring applications, readers gain the skills needed to make a memorable impression and stand out in a competitive job market.

Chapter 5: Excelling in UK Job Interviews

Securing job interviews is a milestone, and chapter five guides readers on excelling in UK job interviews. From understanding common interview formats to showcasing cultural awareness and effectively responding to questions, individuals gain insights into navigating interviews with confidence and professionalism.

Chapter 6: Understanding UK Workplace Culture

Entering the UK workforce involves understanding workplace norms, communication styles, and collaborative approaches. Chapter six explores the nuances of UK workplace culture, providing strategies for effective communication, building professional relationships, and navigating hierarchical structures.

Chapter 7: Leveraging Networking Opportunities

Chapter seven offers a comprehensive guide to leveraging networking opportunities. From joining professional networks to utilising online platforms and attending industry events, readers learn how to build meaningful connections that contribute to their professional growth.

Chapter 8: Overcoming Job Search Challenges

Chapter eight addresses common job search challenges, from visa and work permit issues to coping with rejection. Readers gain strategies for overcoming obstacles, adapting to remote work challenges, and exploring alternative paths such as freelancing and the gig economy.

Chapter 9: Researching and Targeting Industries in the United Kingdom

In chapter nine, readers learn the importance of researching and targeting industries to focus their job search efforts. From identifying growth sectors to researching specific companies, this chapter provides a strategic approach to aligning one's skills with emerging opportunities in the dynamic UK job market.

Chapter 10: Negotiating Job Offers and Advancing Your Career

The guide concludes with chapter ten, focusing on negotiating job offers and advancing careers. Readers gain insights into salary negotiations, evaluating benefits packages, and securing long-term career advancement opportunities. The chapter emphasises the importance of successful onboarding and continued professional development for sustained success.

In summary, this 10-chapter guide equips individuals with a holistic understanding of the UK job market, offering actionable strategies at every stage of the employment journey. From entrepreneurship to job search mastery, cultural awareness, and career advancement, readers are empowered to navigate the intricacies of the UK professional landscape with confidence and strategic insight.

Chapter 1: Deciding Between Self-Employment and Traditional Employment

1. Introduction

The decision between self-employment and traditional employment is a pivotal one that many individuals face at various stages of their careers. Both paths have unique advantages, challenges, risks, and rewards. Chapter One provides a detailed overview to help you make an informed decision based on your personal circumstances, preferences, and aspirations.

2. Understanding Self-Employment

➢ *Definition and Characteristics*

Here, you are the boss, not your employer. Individuals who choose this path are typically responsible for managing all aspects of their business, from client acquisition to financial management.

➢ *Advantages of Self-Employment*
- Flexibility: Self-employed individuals enjoy greater control over their schedules, allowing for a better work-life balance.
- Unlimited Earning Potential: Your earnings are not capped by a fixed salary; they are directly tied to your efforts and the value you provide. Starting is not easy, but you are in charge of your financial freedom.
- Creative Freedom: You have the autonomy to make decisions and implement ideas without the constraints of corporate bureaucracy.
- Tax Benefits: Depending on your jurisdiction, self-employment may offer various tax advantages, including deductions for business-related expenses.

➢ *Challenges of Self-Employment*
- Financial Instability: Income can be unpredictable, especially during the early stages of self-employment.
- Lack of Benefits: Unlike traditional employees, self-employed individuals are responsible for sourcing their health insurance, retirement plans, and other benefits.
- Isolation: If you work by yourself, it may impact your motivation and creativity.
- Administrative Burden: Managing administrative tasks such as invoicing, bookkeeping, and compliance can be time-consuming.

What you have to think of here is to use my personal template to decide what to do next. Remember that these can include both work and hobbies to get you started. Use it as a guidance.

Ten things you're passionate about:	Ten things you love or would like to do:	Ten things I hate or won't do it:
For example, starting my own business	For example, working from home.	For example, working in a noisy environment.
1.		
2.		
3.		
4.		
5.		
6.		
7.		
8.		
9.		
10.		

This exercise will help you understand your needs, as just getting a job you will hate after a few weeks isn't beneficial and might affect your mood.

3. Exploring Traditional Employment

➤ *Definition and Characteristics*

Traditional employment involves working for an employer under a predetermined agreement, often on a full-time or part-time basis. Employees receive a fixed salary or hourly wage and are entitled to various benefits provided by the employer.

➤ *Advantages of Traditional Employment*
- Stability: Traditional employment offers a consistent income, benefits, and a structured work environment.
- Benefits Package: Employees often receive benefits such as health insurance, retirement plans, paid time off, and professional development opportunities.
- Structured Environment: Working within an established organisation provides a framework for growth, mentorship, and collaboration.

- Work-Life Balance: In some roles, employees enjoy predictable work hours and weekends off, allowing for a balanced lifestyle.

➢ *Challenges of Traditional Employment*
- Limited Autonomy: Employees often have less control over their schedules, projects, and decision-making processes.
- Career Progression Constraints: Advancement opportunities may be limited by organisational hierarchy, competition, or other factors.
- Job Security Concerns: No job is secure in today's rapidly changing economy. Downsizing, restructuring, and outsourcing are common challenges.
- Commuting and Location Constraints: Traditional employment means an expensive commute to work, which isn't time or cost-effective.

➢ *Factors to Consider When Making a Decision*
- Personal Preferences – here, you can refer to the personal template I used above.
- Risk Tolerance: Are you comfortable with self-employment's uncertainties and financial risks? Again, you have to be honest, and what worked for me was consulting my family as a part of the process.
- Work Style: Do you thrive in a structured environment, or do you prefer the autonomy and flexibility of self-employment?
- Skill Set: Evaluate your skills, expertise, and interests to determine which path aligns with your strengths and aspirations. Remember that many employers are looking for the skills you already have. Still, you must showcase and make them aware during the application/hiring process.

➢ *Financial Considerations*
- Income Stability: Assess your financial obligations, savings, and risk tolerance to determine how self-employment may impact your financial security.
- Start-up Costs: Consider the initial investment required to launch a business versus the potential return on investment.
- Tax Repercussions: Speak with a tax professional to grasp the tax implications of self-employment versus traditional employment in your jurisdiction.

Tip: I recommend getting free financial advice by arranging an appointment with the Citizen Advice Bureau.

➤ *Lifestyle Considerations*

- Work-Life Balance: Evaluate how each option aligns with your desired lifestyle, including flexibility, work hours, and family commitments.

- Location Independence: Determine if self-employment offers the freedom to work remotely or travel, depending on your preferences.

- Health and Benefits: Consider your healthcare needs, retirement planning (even if you are a younger candidate), and other benefits when comparing self-employment and traditional employment options. For example, by working for either a University or in the Civil Service sector, the employer's pension contribution would yield a higher pension in the long run.

Conclusion

Deciding between self-employment and traditional employment isn't easy and includes personal preferences, financial considerations, and lifestyle goals. While self-employment offers autonomy, flexibility, and unlimited earning potential, it also comes with financial instability, administrative burdens, and other challenges. In contrast, traditional employment provides stability, benefits, and a structured work environment but may limit autonomy and career progression opportunities. Sometimes, like I did in the past, it might be possible to work full-time and also have a side hustle to top up your earnings. Just check your employment contract and any restrictive covenant to avoid doing something that can be seen as a conflict of interest and might put your job at risk. For example, you might be working in the office, and for your side hustle, you start a YouTube channel.

Chapter 2: Identifying Your Skills and Career Goals

Introduction

In today's rapidly evolving job market within the United Kingdom (UK), it's imperative to have a clear understanding of your skills and career aspirations. The modern landscape demands adaptability, continuous learning, and a keen sense of self-awareness. This chapter aims to guide you through the process of identifying your unique skills, understanding the current UK job market trends, and aligning your career goals to ensure success.

Tip: Remember that what worked for you five years ago might not work anymore, so adaptability is a great skill to have or work towards developing one.

1. *Understanding the Current UK Job Market*

➢ Economic Landscape: The UK job market has undergone significant changes, influenced by global events such as Brexit, technological advancements, and the aftermath of the COVID-19 pandemic. Recognising these shifts is crucial to navigating the landscape effectively.

➢ Industry Trends: Various sectors, including technology, healthcare, green energy, and digital marketing, are experiencing growth. Conversely, traditional sectors might be undergoing transformations or decline. It's good to check the job description in depth to ensure you are 100% certain that you want to be considered for that specific job.

➢ Skills in Demand: As industries evolve, so do the skills required. Analytical thinking, digital literacy, adaptability, and soft skills like communication and teamwork are highly valued. You have a lot of free online certifications, for example, language skills, via an app called Duolingo or various certificates that can be completed via Google. Just make sure you read the small print.

2. *Self-Assessment: Identifying Your Skills*

Hard Skills: These are tangible, technical skills acquired through education, training, or work experience. Examples include proficiency in software, data analysis, or specific industry-related certifications.

- ➢ Action Steps:
  - List down your academic qualifications.
    - Identify any specialised training or certifications.
    - Assess technical skills through self-reflection or feedback from friends or family members.

Soft Skills: These are interpersonal or 'people' skills that facilitate effective interactions and relationships. Examples encompass communication, leadership, problem-solving, and emotional intelligence.

- ➢ Action Steps:
  - Reflect on past experiences where you demonstrated leadership or teamwork.
  - Seek feedback from colleagues or mentors about your interpersonal skills.
  - Participate in workshops or training sessions to refine soft skills.

Tip: Both skills mentioned above should be listed on your CV, which we will cover later in this handbook.

Transferable Skills: These are versatile skills that are valuable across various roles and industries. Examples include project management, critical thinking, and time management.

- ➢ Action Steps:
  - Identify experiences from different facets of your life (work, volunteer roles, hobbies) that highlight transferable skills.
  - Translate these skills into relevant contexts for potential employers.

3. *Setting Career Goals*

Short-Term Goals: You aim to achieve these objectives within 1-3 years. They might include acquiring a specific certification, transitioning to a new role within your current organisation, or gaining experience in a particular industry.

- ➢ *Action Steps:*
  - Evaluate your current position and skills.
  - Research opportunities aligned with your interests and skills.

- Develop a timeline and action plan to achieve these goals.

Long-Term Goals: These broader aspirations shape your career trajectory over 3-10 years. Examples could encompass reaching a senior management position, starting your venture, or transitioning into a different industry.

➤ Action Steps:
- To assess your position, you should draft a SWOT analysis (Strengths, Weaknesses, Opportunities, Threats).

This is a template you can use:

Strengths:	Weaknesses:
• • • • • •	• • • • • •
Opportunities:	Threats:
• • • • • •	• • • • • •

- Network with professionals in your desired industry or role. My mentor always says: "Your network is your net worth".

4. *Aligning Skills with Career Goals*

Gap Analysis: Compare your current skills and qualifications with the requirements of your desired roles or industries.

➤ Action Steps:
- Research job descriptions and industry standards.

- Identify skill gaps through self-assessment or professional feedback.
- Invest in relevant training, certifications, or experiences to address these gaps.

Networking and Mentorship: Engage with professionals in your desired field to gain insights, guidance, and opportunities. Mentorship relationships can provide invaluable advice, support, and connections.

  - ➢ Action Steps:
    - Attend industry conferences, seminars, or networking events.
    - Join professional associations or online communities related to your field.
    - Seek mentorship from experienced professionals to navigate challenges and opportunities.

5. *Embracing Continuous Learning and Adaptability*

Lifelong Learning: The dynamic nature of the UK job market necessitates continuous learning and upskilling. Embrace professional development, education, and training opportunities to remain relevant and competitive.

  - ➢ *Action Steps:*
    - Identify areas for improvement or new skills relevant to your industry.
    - Enrol in courses, workshops, or certifications to enhance your knowledge and expertise.
    - Adaptability: Develop resilience, flexibility, and openness to change. Embrace challenges, pivot when necessary, and leverage your skills and experiences to navigate evolving landscapes effectively.
    - Cultivate a growth mindset focused on continuous improvement and adaptability.
    - Embrace feedback, learn from failures, and iterate your strategies.
    - Foster a proactive approach to change, innovation, and emerging opportunities.

Conclusion

Identifying your skills and career goals within the current United Kingdom job market requires introspection, research, and strategic planning. You can navigate the complexities by understanding the economic landscape, assessing your skills, setting clear goals, aligning with industry trends, and embracing continuous learning. Remember, your unique skills, experiences, and aspirations shape your career journey. Stay proactive, adaptable, and committed to growth to succeed in the dynamic UK job market.

Note: This chapter provides an overview of the topic and requires further exploration, research, and personalisation based on individual circumstances, industry specifics, and market dynamics.

Chapter 3: Navigating UK Job Search Platforms

Introduction

In the digital age, job search platforms have revolutionised how individuals explore career opportunities, connect with employers, and navigate the employment landscape. Understanding and effectively utilising these platforms is paramount for those seeking employment within the United Kingdom (UK). This chapter delves deep into navigating UK job search platforms, offering insights, strategies, and best practices to maximise your job search success.

1. *The Evolution of Job Search Platforms in the UK*

- Historical Context: From newspaper classifieds to online job boards and specialised platforms, the evolution of job search mechanisms reflects technological advancements, changing labour dynamics, and evolving employer needs.
- Digital Transformation: The proliferation of internet connectivity, mobile devices, and digital platforms has facilitated real-time access to job opportunities, resources, and networking avenues.
- Diversity of Platforms: Today, UK job seekers can access various platforms ranging from general job boards to niche sites focused on specific industries, roles, or demographics.

2. *Key UK Job Search Platforms: An Overview*

- ➢ General Job Boards:
  - Indeed: One of the largest global job search engines, Indeed aggregates listings from various sources, offering multiple opportunities across sectors and regions.
  - Reed.co.uk: A prominent UK-based job board, Reed provides listings spanning multiple industries, career levels, and geographic locations.
  - Totaljobs: Catering to diverse audiences, Totaljobs offers various roles, resources, and insights tailored to the UK market.

- **CV-Library:** Similar to Totaljobs, it covers almost all sectors the job seeker needs, so again, it's worth a shot.

- ➢ Specialised Platforms:
  - **LinkedIn:** Beyond Networking, LinkedIn is a robust platform for job seekers, employers, and recruiters. Its job search feature, company profiles, and networking capabilities make it indispensable for industry professionals.
  - **CWJobs:** Focused on the IT and tech sectors, CWJobs connects job seekers with opportunities ranging from software development to cybersecurity roles.
  - **Guardian Jobs:** Catering to a more niche audience, Guardian Jobs features roles within sectors such as media, education, arts, and non-profit organisations.

- ➢ **Industry-Specific Platforms:** Depending on your career path, exploring specialised platforms such as NHS Jobs (healthcare), TES (education), or RetailChoice (retail) can provide targeted opportunities and insights.

Tip#1: What was a real game changer for me was to utilise Google Jobs, which pulls all jobs listed online from sites you probably never heard of. You type in the Google search for the desired job, and you must add the bit called near me: for example, for a teaching role, type Education jobs near me. Click on the blue tab that appears in the job search, ignoring all sponsored links. It looks like this:

Tip#2: For job seekers who prefer to work from home, for example, single parents with no childcare or people with mobility issues, you can see the "work-from-home" option under the location. Use this and apply all relevant filters to narrow down the search. I would advise using the "date posted" filter and choosing the "past week" option.

The last tab is called Employers, where you can select a specific employer you wish to work for to narrow the search further.

Tip#3: Don't write off recruitment agencies. If you register with a specialist recruitment agency, they will help you. It's worth explaining how it works: most UK-based companies officially like the doctrine of "try before you buy", hence why they like to engage with recruitment agencies that might interest you in temp to perm roles. Also, the agency will not earn any money until you start working, so leverage their presence as they will work with you and add extra help with interviews and hints for free. You can quickly find them by typing "recruitment agencies near me" in the Google search tab.

3. *Strategies for Effective Job Search Platform Utilisation*

➢ Profile Creation and Optimisation:
- Craft a Compelling Profile: Ensure your CV, cover letter, and profile reflect your skills, experiences, and aspirations concisely and professionally.
- Keywords and SEO: Incorporate relevant keywords, industry-specific terminology, and skills to enhance visibility and alignment with potential employers' criteria.
- Professional Imagery and Branding: Use professional photos, consistent branding, and compelling summaries to create a memorable and authentic online presence.

➢ Advanced Search and Filtering:
- Customise Your Search: Utilise advanced search and filtering options to narrow down opportunities based on criteria such as location, salary, industry, experience level, and company size.
- Set Up Alerts: Create job alerts to receive notifications for relevant opportunities, ensuring timely application and proactive engagement with potential employers.

➢ Networking and Engagement:

- **Connect with Professionals:** Leverage platforms like LinkedIn to network with industry professionals, join groups, participate in discussions, and seek mentorship opportunities.
- **Engage with Content:** Share insights, articles, and updates related to your field, engage with recruiters, and participate in webinars, virtual events, and networking sessions.

➢ Research and Due Diligence:
- **Company Insights:** Research potential employers, company culture, values, and reputation to assess alignment with your career goals, values, and aspirations.

Tip: while it is time-consuming, the work you put in really gives you the advantage as it shows potential employers that you're ready to go the extra mile to work on your profile.

4. Overcoming Challenges and Maximising Opportunities

- **Competitive Landscape:** Recognise the competitive nature of the job market and differentiate yourself through tailored applications, personalised outreach, and value proposition articulation.
- **Adaptability:** Embrace flexibility, adaptability, and resilience amidst uncertainties, market fluctuations, and evolving employer needs. Continuously refine your skills, strategies, and approach to remain competitive and relevant.
- **Feedback and Iteration:** Seek feedback from peers, mentors, and industry professionals to refine your approach, address gaps, and enhance marketability. Iterate your strategies based on insights, experiences, and outcomes to optimise your job search journey.

5. Conclusion and Future Outlook

Navigating UK job search platforms requires a strategic, proactive, and informed approach encompassing profile optimisation, advanced search techniques, Networking, research, and adaptability. You can navigate the dynamic landscape effectively by leveraging diverse platforms, staying abreast of industry trends, engaging with professionals, and continuously refining your strategies.

As technology evolves, labour dynamics shift and market trends fluctuate, staying adaptable, resilient, and proactive remains paramount. Embrace digital transformation, leverage innovative tools and platforms, and position yourself strategically to maximise opportunities, realise your career aspirations, and successfully navigate the UK job market.

Please note that navigating UK job search platforms, encompassing strategies, insights, and best practices, is difficult. However, individual circumstances, industry nuances, and market dynamics may necessitate personalised approaches, further exploration, and continuous adaptation.

Chapter 4: Crafting a Winning UK Resume and Cover Letter

Introduction

In the competitive job landscape of the United Kingdom (UK), your resume and cover letter are crucial tools to capture attention, showcase your qualifications, and differentiate yourself from other candidates. This chapter delves into crafting a compelling UK resume and cover letter, offering insights, strategies, and best practices tailored to resonate with UK employers and recruiters.

Understanding the UK Resume: A Comprehensive Overview

This is a very important and probably the main reason why your CV won't get you shortlisted for the interview.

Writing a UK CV That Will Pass the ATS (Applicant Tracking System)

Apologies if this chapter seems too technical, but it is for your benefit, so I hope you'll understand.

In today's digital recruitment landscape, Applicant Tracking Systems (ATS) are widely utilised by UK employers to streamline recruitment, manage applications, and efficiently identify qualified candidates. To ensure your CV successfully navigates through ATS algorithms and reaches human eyes, it's essential to understand ATS functionalities, optimise your CV accordingly, and adhere to best practices. This guide outlines strategies and insights to craft a UK CV tailored for ATS compatibility and human readability.

---

1. *Understanding ATS: Key Components and Functions*
   - Parsing Technology: ATS software employs parsing technology to scan, categorise, and analyse CVs based on specific criteria, keywords, formatting, and

relevancy. Understanding ATS algorithms, filters, and functionalities is crucial to optimising your CV effectively.

- Keyword Matching: ATS systems identify relevant keywords, phrases, skills, qualifications, and experiences aligned with job descriptions, requirements, and employer criteria. Incorporating targeted keywords strategically enhances visibility and alignment with ATS algorithms.
- Formatting and Structure: ATS software evaluates CV formatting, structure, layout, headings, subheadings, fonts, bullet points, and consistency. Adhering to ATS-friendly formatting guidelines ensures accurate parsing, categorisation, and analysis of your CV content.

---

2. Crafting an ATS-Compatible UK CV: Strategies and Best Practices

Tip: Use the following command in the Google search tab: "ats cv template free download word."

- ➤ Keyword Integration and Optimisation:
    - Analyse Job Descriptions: Review job descriptions, requirements, qualifications, and responsibilities to identify relevant keywords, skills, experiences, and qualifications. Tailor your CV content to incorporate targeted keywords naturally within context, sections, and bullet points.
    - Strategic Placement: Integrate keywords strategically within the CV's professional summary, skills section, experience descriptions, achievements, qualifications, and additional sections relevant to the role, industry, and employer expectations.
    - Avoid Keyword Stuffing: Maintain a balanced approach by incorporating relevant keywords naturally, authentically, and contextually. Avoid excessive repetition, redundancy, or unnatural keyword placement that compromises readability, coherence, and authenticity.

- ➤ Formatting and Structure Optimisation:
    - Use ATS-Compatible Templates: Utilise CV templates designed for ATS compatibility, readability, and parsing accuracy. Avoid complex designs, graphics, images, headers, footers, tables, columns, or unconventional formatting elements that may hinder ATS parsing, analysis, or categorisation.
    - Consistent Formatting: Maintain consistent formatting, layout, headings, subheadings, fonts, bullet points, dates, and styling throughout the CV. Use

standard section headings (e.g., Professional Experience, Education, Skills, Certifications) to facilitate ATS recognition, categorisation, and analysis.

- **Avoid Embedded Elements:** Exclude embedded elements, graphics, charts, tables, images, logos, or non-text elements that may disrupt ATS parsing, categorisation, or processing. Focus on textual content, clarity, coherence, and ATS-friendly formatting elements to enhance compatibility and readability.

> Content Clarity, Relevance, and Authenticity:

- **Tailored Content:** Customise your CV content to align with specific roles, industries, employers, and ATS criteria. Highlight relevant experiences, achievements, skills, qualifications, and insights demonstrating your alignment, value proposition, and fit for the role.

- **Clear and Concise Language:** Use clear, concise, professional language, bullet points, action verbs, and statements to convey information, accomplishments, responsibilities, contributions, and outcomes effectively: Prioritise relevance, authenticity, coherence, and clarity to engage ATS systems and resonate with recruiters.

---

3. Testing and Optimising Your ATS-Compatible UK CV

- **ATS Compatibility Tools:** Utilise ATS compatibility tools, software, platforms, or services available online to evaluate your CV's compatibility, readability, parsing accuracy, and alignment with ATS algorithms. These tools provide insights, feedback, recommendations, and guidance to effectively refine your approach, content, and strategy.

- **Tailored Applications:** Customise your CV for each application by analysing job descriptions, requirements, qualifications, and employer expectations. Tailor your CV content, keywords, skills, experiences, and insights to align with specific roles, industries, employers, and ATS criteria.

- **Continuous Learning and Adaptation:** Stay abreast of ATS trends, technologies, updates, functionalities, best practices, and insights within the UK recruitment landscape. Continuously refine, adapt, and optimise your CV strategy, content, formatting, and approach based on feedback, experiences, outcomes, and opportunities.

Conclusion about the ATS

Crafting an ATS-compatible UK CV requires strategic planning, keyword optimisation, formatting adherence, content clarity, relevance, authenticity, and continuous refinement. Understanding ATS functionalities, best practices, guidelines, and insights can enhance visibility, engagement, compatibility, and success within the competitive UK job market. Prioritise alignment with employer expectations, role requirements, industry trends, and ATS criteria to effectively differentiate yourself, capture attention, and secure opportunities.

Now, let's move to a more comprehensive overview of your CV.

➢ Structure and Format: Unlike CVs, which can be more detailed and extensive, UK resumes (often referred to as "CVs" within the UK context) are typically concise, focused, and tailored to specific roles. A standard UK resume spans 1-2 pages, highlighting relevant experience, skills, achievements, and qualifications.

➢ Key Components:
  • Personal Details: Name, contact information (phone number, professional email), and LinkedIn profile (if applicable). **The latter is very important as most employers will try to learn more about you, so visiting your LinkedIn profile would happen nine out of ten times!**
  • Professional Summary or Objective: A concise overview highlighting your professional background, expertise, career aspirations, and value proposition.
  • Professional Experience: Chronologically listing relevant roles, organisations, dates, responsibilities, achievements, and quantifiable results.
  • Education and Qualifications: Academic credentials, institutions, graduation dates, relevant coursework, certifications, and additional training.
  • Skills: Highlight key technical, transferable, and soft skills relevant to the desired role, industry, and employer requirements.
  • Achievements and Awards: Showcase significant accomplishments, recognitions, certifications, publications, or relevant affiliations.

2. Crafting a Compelling UK Resume: Strategies and Best Practices

  • Tailoring and Customisation:

- Research and Alignment: Analyse job descriptions, company culture, values, and requirements to tailor your resume accordingly. Align your qualifications, experiences, and achievements with specific roles, industries, and employer expectations.
- Highlight Relevance: Prioritise and emphasise relevant experiences, skills, achievements, and qualifications. Focus on outcomes, impact, and contributions, demonstrating your value proposition and alignment with the role's requirements.

- Clarity and Conciseness:
  - Brevity and Precision: Maintain clarity, conciseness, and relevance. Use concise language, bullet points, action verbs, and quantifiable results to convey information effectively. Avoid jargon, redundancies, and irrelevant details.

- Formatting and Design:
  - Ensure consistency in formatting, layout, fonts, and styling. Use professional templates, headings, subheadings, and spacing to enhance readability, aesthetics, and impact.

- Quantifiable Achievements and Results:
  - Showcase Impact: Quantify achievements, results, contributions, and outcomes using metrics, percentages, numbers, or tangible examples. Highlight challenges, solutions, innovations, and results that showcase your capabilities, contributions, and value proposition.
  - Action-Oriented Language: Utilise action verbs, dynamic language, and results-driven statements to convey accomplishments, initiatives, leadership, collaboration, and problem-solving abilities.

---

3. Crafting a Persuasive UK Cover Letter: Strategies and Best Practices

Tip: not all employers ask for a cover letter, but I'd advise personalising your cover letter the same as your CV for EACH ROLE you apply for, as it will score high on the ATS score.

- Personalisation and Customisation:

- Addressing and Salutation: Personalise cover letters by addressing specific individuals (e.g., hiring managers, recruiters) whenever possible. Research and identify key contacts, roles, and departments.

- Introduction: Begin with a compelling introduction that captures attention, establishes rapport, and conveys enthusiasm for the role, organisation, and industry.

- Crafting a Compelling Cover Letter for UK Applications:

The cover letter is an integral part of job applications in the UK, allowing candidates to express their motivations and qualifications. This section explores the components of an effective cover letter, guiding readers on how to structure their letters and tailor content to specific roles. Emphasis is placed on articulating a genuine interest in the company and aligning one's skills with the job requirements.

- Showcasing Fit and Alignment:

Alignment with Role and Organisation: Align your qualifications, experiences, achievements, skills, and aspirations with the role's requirements, organisation's culture, values, mission, and objectives. Demonstrate a clear understanding of the role, industry trends, challenges, and opportunities.

- Highlighting Value Proposition and Contribution:
  - Articulate Value: Clearly articulate your value proposition, unique selling points, strengths, expertise, and contributions. Highlight relevant experiences, accomplishments, skills, and insights that differentiate you and position you as a valuable asset to the organisation.
  - Demonstrate Passion and Enthusiasm: Convey genuine passion, enthusiasm, motivation, and alignment with the organisation's mission, values, culture, and objectives. Showcase your commitment, dedication, curiosity, and proactive approach to contributing, innovating, and driving results.

- Professionalism and Tone:

- Maintain Professionalism: Use formal language, tone, structure, and conventions. Proofread meticulously for grammar, spelling, punctuation, clarity, coherence, and consistency. Ensure adherence to guidelines, requirements, and industry standards.
- Conciseness and Focus: Maintain brevity, focus, and relevance. Avoid repetition, verbosity, generic statements, clichés, and irrelevant details. Ensure clarity, impact, and alignment with the role, organisation, and industry nuances.

---

4. Conclusion and Action Steps

Crafting a winning UK resume and cover letter requires strategic planning, research, customisation, alignment, clarity, professionalism, and attention to detail. By understanding the UK job market, employer expectations, role requirements, industry trends, and best practices, you can effectively differentiate yourself, capture attention, showcase your value proposition, and secure opportunities.

- Action Steps:
  - Conduct comprehensive research on target roles, industries, organisations, and trends.
  - Analyse job descriptions, requirements, expectations, and alignment factors.
  - Tailor, customise, and optimise your resume and cover letter for specific opportunities.
  - Seek feedback, insights, guidance, and support from mentors, peers, professionals, and resources.
  - Continuously refine, iterate, and adapt your strategies, approach, and materials based on feedback, experiences, outcomes, and opportunities.

Note: We discussed crafting a winning UK resume and cover letter encompassing strategies, insights, and best practices. However, individual circumstances, industry nuances, role specifics, and market dynamics may necessitate personalised approaches, further exploration, continuous adaptation, and expert guidance.

Chapter 5: Excelling in UK Job Interviews

Introduction

Securing a job interview in the United Kingdom (UK) is a significant milestone, but excelling in the interview process is crucial to land your desired role. The UK job market is competitive, and candidates must demonstrate a combination of skills, preparation, professionalism, and cultural awareness to stand out. This chapter provides comprehensive insights, strategies, and best practices to excel in UK job interviews, ensuring you present yourself effectively, confidently, and authentically. Good luck!

1. Understanding the UK Job Interview Landscape

- Types of Interviews: In the UK, job interviews can encompass various formats, including:
  - Traditional Face-to-Face Interviews: Direct interaction with interviewers at the company's location.
  - Virtual/Remote Interviews: Conducted via video conferencing platforms, telephone, or online tools.
  - Panel Interviews: Involving multiple interviewers or panel members representing different departments, roles, or perspectives.
  - Competency-Based Interviews: Focusing on specific skills, experiences, competencies, scenarios, or behavioural attributes relevant to the role.
  - Cultural Considerations: Recognise and adapt to UK cultural norms, etiquette, communication styles, professionalism, and interview expectations. Embrace

punctuality, politeness, respect, integrity, and cultural sensitivity throughout the interview process.

---

2. Preparation: Key Components for Success

- Research and Due Diligence:
  - Company Insights: Conduct comprehensive research on the company, industry, culture, values, mission, vision, products, services, competitors, recent news, challenges, opportunities, and market trends. To gather insights leverage company websites, annual reports, press releases, social media platforms, industry publications, and networking avenues.
  - Role Understanding: Analyse the job description, requirements, responsibilities, expectations, qualifications, skills, competencies, and alignment with your background, expertise, aspirations, and career goals.

- Self-Assessment and Reflection:
  - Skills and Experiences: Reflect on your skills, experiences, achievements, qualifications, strengths, weaknesses, growth areas, challenges, solutions, contributions, and value proposition. Prepare tangible examples, stories, scenarios, or anecdotes demonstrating your capabilities, accomplishments, and alignment with the role.
  - Personal Branding: Define your personal brand, unique selling points, passions, values, aspirations, motivations, professional identity, and cultural fit. Craft a compelling narrative, elevator pitch, or value proposition highlighting your distinctiveness, authenticity, and alignment with the organisation's culture, objectives, and expectations.

- Mock Interviews and Preparation:
  - Practice and Rehearsal: Engage in mock interviews, role-playing, practice sessions, or simulations to refine your responses, articulation, confidence, body language, tone, timing, and presentation skills. Solicit feedback, insights, guidance, and recommendations from mentors, peers, professionals, or career experts to enhance your preparation, performance, and readiness.
  - Questions Preparation: Anticipate and prepare for potential interview questions, scenarios, challenges, or topics, including:

- Technical Questions: Assessing your industry-specific knowledge, expertise, skills, experiences, or qualifications.
- Behavioural Questions: Evaluate your competencies, problem-solving abilities, teamwork, leadership, communication, adaptability, resilience, and cultural fit.
- Situational Questions: Presenting hypothetical scenarios, challenges, dilemmas, or case studies relevant to the role, industry, organisation, or professional context.

3. Excelling During the Interview: Strategies and Best Practices

- Professionalism and Etiquette:
  - Punctuality and Preparation: Arrive early, prepared, organised, and equipped with necessary documents, materials, attire, and mindset. Demonstrate respect, enthusiasm, commitment, dedication, and professionalism throughout the interview process.
  - Dress Code and Appearance: Adhere to industry-specific dress codes, norms, expectations, and cultural standards. Present yourself professionally, appropriately, and authentically, considering company culture, role requirements, interview format, and industry nuances.

- Communication and Engagement:
  - Active Listening: Listen attentively, actively, and empathetically to interviewers' questions, insights, feedback, expectations, and perspectives. Clarify uncertainties, seek clarification, demonstrate understanding, and engage in meaningful, respectful, and constructive dialogue.
  - Articulation and Clarity: Communicate clearly, concisely, confidently, and coherently using appropriate language, tone, structure, and content. Showcase your communication skills, interpersonal abilities, cultural awareness, emotional intelligence, and professional insight effectively.

- Authenticity and Alignment:
  - Genuine Responses: Respond authentically, genuinely, and transparently to interview questions, scenarios, challenges, or topics. Share honest insights,

experiences, perspectives, reflections, motivations, aspirations, and contributions without exaggeration, fabrication, or misrepresentation.

- Cultural Fit and Alignment: Emphasise your alignment with the organisation's culture, values, mission, vision, objectives, expectations, and industry norms. Showcase your passion, enthusiasm, commitment, dedication, adaptability, resilience, and potential contributions effectively.

- Confidence and Resilience:
  - Positive Mindset: Maintain a positive, optimistic, proactive, resilient, and adaptive mindset throughout the interview. Embrace challenges, uncertainties, feedback, opportunities, and experiences with confidence, determination, curiosity, openness, and growth orientation.
  - Feedback and Reflection: Solicit feedback, insights, recommendations, or guidance from interviewers, mentors, peers, professionals, or experts post-interview. Reflect on your performance, responses, experiences, emotions, challenges, opportunities, outcomes, and learnings to enhance your preparation, strategies, approaches, and future performance.

Tip: Always ask panel two or a maximum of three questions at the end of the interview. What worked for me was asking questions that underline your interest in the job. For example:

- How many interview stages did the panel prepare for, and what timeframe is expected to receive feedback?
- How crucial is this role for your potential Line Manager?
- What makes it such a great place to work?
- Is there a career progression for committed employees?

4. Conclusion and Action Steps

Excelling in UK job interviews necessitates strategic preparation, professionalism, communication, engagement, authenticity, alignment, confidence, resilience, and continuous learning. By understanding the UK job market landscape, cultural considerations, interview dynamics, employer expectations, role requirements, industry nuances, and best practices, you can effectively differentiate yourself, captivate interviewers, demonstrate value, and secure opportunities.

- Action Steps:

- Conduct comprehensive research on target companies, industries, roles, and market trends.
- Analyse job descriptions, requirements, responsibilities, skills, competencies, and alignment factors.
- Reflect on your skills, experiences, achievements, values, aspirations, strengths, weaknesses, challenges, and growth areas.
- Engage in mock interviews, practice sessions, role-playing, or simulations to refine your preparation, responses, articulation, confidence, and presentation skills.
- Solicit feedback, insights, recommendations, guidance, or support from mentors, peers, professionals, experts, or resources.
- Continuously refine, adapt, iterate, and enhance your strategies, approaches, techniques, insights, knowledge, skills, and performance based on experiences, feedback, outcomes, challenges, opportunities, trends, and developments.

Note: Here, we covered excelling in UK job interviews, encompassing insights, strategies, best practices, considerations, and action steps. Individual circumstances, industry specifics, role nuances, cultural dynamics, interview dynamics, and market trends may necessitate personalised approaches, further exploration, continuous adaptation, and expert guidance.

Chapter 6: Understanding UK Workplace Culture

Introduction

Navigating the intricate fabric of the UK workplace culture requires understanding its history, values, etiquette, communication styles, and unwritten rules. With a blend of tradition and modernity, the UK workplace offers a unique blend of professionalism, collaboration, and respect. This chapter delves deep into the nuances, characteristics, and dynamics of the UK workplace culture, providing insights, strategies, and best practices for seamless integration and success.

1. *Historical Context and Evolution*
   - Industrial Revolution: The UK's rich industrial history significantly shaped its work culture, emphasising productivity, innovation, efficiency, and growth. The legacy of industrialisation continues to influence work ethics, practices, values, and dynamics within modern organisations.
   - Colonial Legacy: The UK's colonial past introduced diverse cultural influences, global perspectives, collaboration models, communication styles, and business practices. Embracing multiculturalism, diversity, inclusion, and globalisation remains integral to the UK workplace culture.

- Economic Shifts: From manufacturing to services, finance, technology, healthcare, education, and creative industries, the UK's economic evolution diversifies work environments, roles, skills, expectations, and opportunities. Adapting to industry trends, innovations, disruptions, and transformations shapes workplace dynamics, competitiveness, and sustainability.

2. *Key Characteristics of UK Workplace Culture*
   - Professionalism: Upholding professionalism, integrity, ethics, responsibility, accountability, transparency, diligence, and commitment remains paramount. Demonstrating reliability, consistency, punctuality, and dedication fosters trust, credibility, respect, and collaboration within teams and organisations.
   - Communication Styles: Embracing direct, clear, concise, polite, respectful, and articulate communication enhances understanding, collaboration, engagement, alignment, and effectiveness. Balancing assertiveness with diplomacy, empathy, active listening, feedback, and openness promotes constructive dialogue, innovation, problem-solving, and relationship-building.
   - Teamwork and Collaboration: Valuing teamwork, collaboration, cooperation, synergy, inclusivity, and collective contributions fosters a collaborative, supportive, cohesive, and unified work environment. Encouraging diversity, perspectives, ideas, insights, skills, experiences, and backgrounds enhances creativity, innovation, adaptability, and competitiveness.
   - Hierarchy and Structure: Acknowledging organisational hierarchy, structure, authority, responsibility, roles, and decision-making processes promotes clarity, alignment, direction, accountability, efficiency, and effectiveness. Respecting seniority, expertise, experience, leadership, and contributions fosters respect, recognition, mentorship, growth, and development.
   - Work-Life Balance: Prioritising work-life balance, well-being, mental health, flexibility, autonomy, and personalisation acknowledges individual needs, preferences, priorities, motivations, aspirations, and commitments. Embracing flexibility, adaptability, support, understanding, and empathy enhances productivity, satisfaction, engagement, retention, and loyalty.

3. *Cultural Nuances and Etiquette*
   - Punctuality: Adhering to punctuality, deadlines, schedules, and timelines demonstrates respect, professionalism, reliability, commitment, and efficiency.

Arriving on time for meetings, appointments, engagements, and responsibilities fosters trust, credibility, collaboration, and productivity.

- Professional Attire: Embracing appropriate attire, presentation, and appearance aligns with organisational culture, industry norms, expectations, roles, responsibilities, and environments. Demonstrating professionalism, respect, authenticity, and alignment enhances credibility, confidence, perception, and engagement.

- Networking and Relationship Building: Engaging in Networking, relationship building, collaboration, mentorship, sponsorship, and community involvement fosters connections, partnerships, opportunities, insights, growth, recognition, and success. Building genuine, meaningful, mutually beneficial relationships enhances collaboration, innovation, support, and advancement.

- Feedback and Development: Embracing constructive feedback, coaching, mentoring, development, learning, growth, improvement, innovation, and continuous improvement promotes excellence, performance, adaptability, resilience, agility, and success.

4. *Embracing Diversity, Inclusion, and Multiculturalism*

- Diversity and Inclusion: Promoting diversity, inclusion, equity, representation, belonging, acceptance, respect, empowerment, and representation fosters innovation, creativity, collaboration, engagement, satisfaction, retention, performance, competitiveness, and success. Valuing diverse perspectives, experiences, skills, and contributions enhances resilience, agility, adaptability, and sustainability.

- Multiculturalism: Celebrating multiculturalism, global perspectives, international collaborations, partnerships, networks, insights, experiences, innovations, and contributions enriches organisations, communities, industries, economies, societies, and ecosystems. Embracing globalisation, intercultural competence, communication, collaboration, awareness, understanding, respect, empathy, curiosity, openness, and adaptability fosters unity, integration, harmony, growth, development, and prosperity.

5. *Conclusion and Action Steps*

Understanding the UK workplace culture requires embracing its history, values, etiquette, communication styles, characteristics, nuances, dynamics, diversity, inclusion, multiculturalism, and evolution. By acknowledging cultural considerations, norms, expectations, dynamics, nuances, challenges, opportunities, and best practices, you can navigate, integrate, contribute, succeed, and thrive within the UK's diverse, dynamic, competitive, innovative, and collaborative work environments.

- Action Steps:
  - Reflect on your cultural awareness, understanding, experiences, perspectives, biases, values, motivations, aspirations, skills, competencies, growth areas, challenges, opportunities, and contributions.
  - Engage in cultural competence training, workshops, seminars, programs, resources, tools, assessments, experiences, and initiatives to enhance your awareness, knowledge, skills, and effectiveness.
  - Foster relationships, connections, collaborations, partnerships, networks, mentorships, sponsorships, engagements, and interactions with diverse individuals, communities, organisations, industries, cultures, societies, and ecosystems.
  - Embrace continuous learning, development, growth, improvement, feedback, reflection, adaptation, innovation, creativity, resilience, agility, and excellence to navigate, integrate, contribute, succeed, and thrive within the UK's diverse, dynamic, competitive, innovative, and collaborative work environments.

Note: We covered the UK workplace culture, encompassing insights, strategies, best practices, considerations, nuances, dynamics, characteristics, and action steps. Individual circumstances, experiences, perspectives, roles, industries, organisations, cultures, environments, and expectations may necessitate personalised approaches, further exploration, continuous adaptation, expert guidance, and cultural competence development.

Chapter 7: Leveraging Networking Opportunities

Introduction

Networking transcends mere interactions; it's a strategic approach to building mutually beneficial relationships, expanding horizons, and unlocking opportunities. In the dynamic landscape of the modern world, Networking serves as a cornerstone for professional growth, personal development, and organisational success. This chapter unravels the intricacies, strategies, tools, and best practices of leveraging networking opportunities effectively, ensuring meaningful connections, collaborations, insights, opportunities, and advancements.

1. *Understanding Networking: Beyond Traditional Perspectives*
   - Definition and Scope: Networking encompasses building, nurturing, maintaining, and leveraging relationships with diverse individuals, groups, communities, and stakeholders. It transcends traditional boundaries and functions, fostering connectivity and prosperity.

   - Evolution and Dynamics: Networking has evolved from conventional interactions to encompass digital platforms, virtual environments, global ecosystems, diverse communities, and advancements.

   - Purpose and Value: Networking serves multiple purposes, including:

- Knowledge Sharing: Exchanging insights, experiences, challenges, solutions, best practices, resources, tools, techniques, and opportunities.

- Collaboration: Partnering, collaborating, co-creating, co-innovating, co-developing, co-delivering, co-solving, and co-succeeding on initiatives, projects, events, and engagements.

- Career Advancement: Expanding professional networks, connections, opportunities, roles, responsibilities, and achievements.

- Personal Development: Enhancing interpersonal skills, communication abilities, emotional intelligence, cultural competence and lifelong learning.

2. *Strategies for Effective Networking*

- Define Objectives and Goals: Clarify your networking objectives, goals, motivations, and outcomes. Establishing clear, specific, measurable, achievable, relevant, time-bound, and aligned goals guides your networking efforts.

- Identify Target Networks: Identify, research, analyse, evaluate, and prioritise targets, partnerships, and opportunities aligned with your objectives, opportunities, and growth areas.

- Build Authentic Relationships: Focus on building authentic, genuine, meaningful, respectful, trust-based, value-driven, reciprocal, sustainable, long-term, and mutually beneficial relationships.

- Leverage Digital Platforms: Embrace digital networking platforms, tools, networks, and resources to expand your reach, visibility, and impact globally.

- Engage Proactively and Responsibly: Actively participate and engage in networking events, conferences, partnerships, discussions, interactions, and opportunities.

3. *Maximising Networking Opportunities*

- **Attend Relevant Events**: Identify, research, evaluate, select, and attend relevant networking events, conferences, and opportunities aligned with your objectives, goals, interests, opportunities, and growth areas.

- **Engage in Professional Development**: Invest in professional development, education, training, certifications, qualifications, and opportunities to enhance your skills, knowledge, expertise, and marketability.

- **Utilise Referrals and Recommendations**: Leverage referrals, recommendations, introductions, connections, endorsements, collaborations, partnerships, and networks.

- **Maintain Relationships**: Nurture, maintain, and revitalise relationships with diverse individuals, communities, and organisations.

4. *Overcoming Challenges and Navigating Complexities*

Strategies for Overcoming Challenges

Embrace a Progress Attitude:

- You must believe self-development will happen if you apply enough effort and stay motivated when others won't. See obstacles as opportunities rather than negative things.

Develop Resistance:

- Being resistant allows you to get back on your feet quicker than others. Cultivate resilience by building a strong support network, practising self-care, and reframing negative experiences as learning opportunities.

Set Clear Goals and Prioritise:

- Break down larger challenges into smaller, manageable tasks. Set clear, actionable goals and prioritise them based on their impact and urgency.

Seek Feedback and Adapt:

- Regularly solicit feedback from mentors, peers, or trusted advisors. You will only learn from the feedback and what you do with it.

5. Conclusion

Note: Here, we covered leveraging networking opportunities, encompassing insights, strategies, best practices, considerations, complexities, challenges and opportunities.

Chapter 8: Overcoming Job Search Challenges

Overcoming Job Search Challenges in the Great Britain.

Introduction

Let's face it: it will be competitive, but possible. While the UK offers many opportunities across various sectors, the journey to securing a position can be riddled with challenges. This chapter delves into some of the most common hurdles job seekers face in the UK and provides actionable strategies to overcome them.

Understanding the Landscape

a. Brexit and its Implications: The UK's decision to leave the European Union has affected its job market. Companies have adjusted their hiring strategies, and there might be changes in work permits and visas. Keeping abreast of immigration policies and understanding how they impact your job search is crucial.

b. Local vs. Global Companies: While multinational corporations offer diverse roles, local companies can provide a more intimate work environment. Decide which aligns with your career goals and tailor your search accordingly.

Crafting an Effective CV and Cover Letter

a. Tailoring your CV: A generic CV seldom catches attention. Tailor your CV for each role by highlighting relevant skills, experiences, and achievements.

b. Personalising the Cover Letter: Use the cover letter as an opportunity to express genuine interest in the company and role. Showcase your passion, skills, and how you can add value.

Tip: This is a must-do – your CV and cover letter should be tailored to each job description.

Networking in the Digital Age

a. LinkedIn and Professional Networking: Maintain an updated LinkedIn profile. Engage with industry professionals, join relevant groups, and participate in discussions. Networking events, both virtual and physical, can also be invaluable.

Tip: if you don't have a LinkedIn profile, I strongly advise you to set one up. There are many instructional videos on YouTube on how to set up your LinkedIn for free.

b. Informational Interviews: Reach out to professionals in your desired field for informational interviews. This not only provides insights but also expands your network.

Navigating Interviews and Assessment Centers

a. Preparing for Interviews: Research the company, its culture, values, and recent developments. Practice common interview questions and be ready with examples showcasing your skills and experiences.

Tip: This is important as many interview questions start with: "What do you know about our company?" or "What attracted you to apply for this role?".

b. Assessment Centers: For roles that involve assessment centres, prepare for group activities, presentations, and case studies. Showcase teamwork, leadership, and problem-solving skills.

Upskilling and Continuous Learning

a. Recognising Skill Gaps: Identify areas where you lack expertise or knowledge. Invest time in acquiring new skills through courses, workshops, or certifications.

b. Staying Relevant: Industries evolve rapidly, hence why continuous learning enhances your employability.

Chapter 9: Researching and Targeting Industries in the United Kingdom

Introduction

A strategic approach is paramount for active job seekers in the dynamic landscape of the United Kingdom's job market. One of the fundamental strategies involves researching and targeting specific industries. Understanding industry nuances, trends, and demands makes you a more informed and attractive candidate. This chapter delves into the methodologies and considerations for researching and targeting industries effectively.

1. Importance of Industry Research

a. Aligning with Personal Goals:

Before diving into industry research, introspect and align your career aspirations, skills, and interests. This alignment ensures that you target industries aligning with your professional goals.

b. Enhancing Job Search Efficiency:

Targeting specific industries streamlines your job search process. Instead of scattering efforts across sectors, a focused approach increases the likelihood of securing relevant opportunities.

2. Methodologies for Industry Research

a. Utilising Online Resources:

- Industry Reports: Websites like Statista, IBISWorld, and MarketResearch.com provide comprehensive industry reports detailing market trends, growth projections, and challenges.
- Government Publications: UK government websites offer sector-specific insights, policy changes, and regulatory updates.
- Industry Blogs and Publications: Follow industry-specific blogs, journals, and magazines for expert insights, analyses, and news.

b. Networking:

- Engage with professionals within target industries. Platforms like LinkedIn facilitate connections with industry experts, allowing for informational interviews, mentorship, and firsthand insights.

c. Attending Industry Events:

- Take part In activities like seminars related to target industries. These events foster networking opportunities, provide industry overviews, and facilitate interactions with industry leaders.

3. Key Considerations for Targeting Industries

a. Growth Potential:

- Evaluate industries with promising growth trajectories. Emerging sectors often present abundant opportunities, reduced competition, and innovative environments.

b. Skill Relevance:

- Assess your skills, qualifications, and experiences concerning industry demands. Target industries are valuing your expertise, facilitating seamless integration and career progression.

c. Cultural Fit:

- Consider industry cultures, values, and work environments. Align with industries reflecting your values, work preferences, and professional aspirations.

d. Economic Indicators:

- Monitor economic indicators influencing industries. Factors like GDP growth, unemployment rates, and consumer spending patterns offer insights into industry stability and growth potential.

4. Tailoring Applications and Approaches

a. Customising CV and Cover Letter:

Tailor CVs and cover letters highlighting relevant experiences, skills, and achievements pertinent to target industries. Emphasise industry-specific knowledge, accomplishments, and contributions.

b. Leveraging Transferable Skills:

Identify transferable skills applicable across industries. Emphasise skills like communication, problem-solving, leadership, and adaptability, positioning yourself as a versatile candidate.

c. Engaging in Industry-specific Training:

Undertake industry-specific courses, certifications, or workshops. Enhancing industry knowledge and skills amplifies credibility, competence, and employability within target sectors.

Conclusion

Researching and targeting industries in the United Kingdom as an active job seeker necessitates diligence, strategy, and adaptability. By employing comprehensive research methodologies, considering key industry factors, and tailoring applications and approaches, you enhance your competitive edge, optimise opportunities, and navigate the UK's job market confidently and effectively.

Embrace the journey, remain proactive, and leverage industry insights to propel your career aspirations in the vibrant landscape of the United Kingdom.

Chapter 10: Negotiating Job Offers and Advancing Your Career

Introduction

It is a great achievement if you land a job offer, but the journey doesn't end there. Effective negotiation ensures that the terms align with your skills, experience, and market value. Furthermore, once onboarded, continuous career advancement remains pivotal. This chapter elucidates strategies for negotiating job offers. It provides insights for propelling your career forward within the UK's professional landscape.

1. Understanding the UK Job Market Dynamics

a. Recognising Industry Standards: Research industry-specific salary benchmarks, benefits, and expectations. Understanding prevailing standards empowers informed negotiation and sets realistic expectations.

b. Economic Considerations: Monitor economic trends, inflation rates, and market demands. Economic fluctuations influence salary structures, bonuses, and benefits, necessitating adaptability and awareness.

---

2. Strategies for Negotiating Job Offers

a. Comprehensive Research:

- Salary Benchmarks: Utilise platforms like Glassdoor, Payscale, and LinkedIn Salary Insights to gauge industry-specific salary ranges.

- Benefits and Perks: Evaluate non-monetary benefits, including healthcare, retirement plans, vacation days, professional development opportunities, and flexible work arrangements.

b. Prioritising Needs and Preferences: Identify essential priorities, be it salary, work-life balance, career growth opportunities, or job responsibilities. Prioritising facilitates focused negotiation, emphasising crucial aspects aligning with personal and professional aspirations.

Tip: only apply for the roles you could see doing for a long time unless you need any role.

c. Effective Communication:

- Articulating Value Proposition: Clearly articulate your value proposition, emphasising skills, experiences, accomplishments, and contributions.

- Open Dialogue: Foster transparent communication, addressing concerns, clarifying expectations, and negotiating mutually beneficial terms.

d. Evaluating Total Compensation: Consider total compensation beyond base salary, encompassing bonuses, commissions, equity options, pension contributions, and additional perks. A holistic evaluation ensures comprehensive understanding and negotiation efficacy.

3. Advancing Your Career in the UK

a. Continuous Learning and Development:

- Skill Enhancement: Identify emerging trends, technologies, and industry developments. Invest in courses, certifications, workshops, and seminars, augmenting expertise and competence.

- Mentorship and Networking: Engage with industry professionals, mentors, and peers. Foster meaningful relationships, seek guidance mentorship, and leverage networking opportunities for career progression.

b. Demonstrating Value and Initiative:

- Proactive Approach: Demonstrate initiative, innovation, and commitment. Volunteer for challenging projects, showcase leadership, problem-solving, and teamwork skills, and consistently deliver exemplary results.

- Seeking Feedback: Solicit constructive feedback, evaluate performance, identify areas of improvement, and leverage insights for professional development and growth.

c. Navigating Organisational Culture:

- Cultural Alignment: Align with organisational values, mission, and culture. Embrace collaboration, diversity, and inclusion, and contribute to fostering positive work environments.

- Visibility and Advocacy: Position yourself as a valuable asset, advocate for recognition advancement opportunities, and engage in initiatives aligning with organisational objectives and growth trajectories.

Conclusion

Negotiating job offers and advancing your career within the UK necessitates strategic planning, effective communication, and continuous growth. You navigate the professional landscape with confidence, resilience, and ambition by understanding market dynamics, prioritising needs, fostering open dialogue, and embracing learning, development, and collaboration opportunities.

Embrace challenges, leverage insights, cultivate relationships, and propel your career aspirations, contributing to personal growth, organisational success, and the dynamic evolution of the UK's professional landscape.

GOOD LUCK!

If you found this guide useful, I would appreciate it if you could leave a positive review –
thank you!